Shining Hard

Anna Farley

Also by Anna Farley:

Reflection of You

Still a Dreamer

Clarity

More Than Love

It takes honesty,
It takes acceptance;
It takes excitement
That gets renewed daily;
It takes respect,
It takes real freedom;
It takes saying the hard things,
And listening deeply.
It takes a desire to be faithful,
A need to keep no secrets.
It takes a true and real love,
But to make it last,
It takes more than love.

Nothing Left
In the end
I hope I'm spent.
That I've played my cards
In the best game I could have.
That I'm weary,
That I've given it all.
I hope I've exhausted
Every resource,
Every bit of energy,
Every ounce of my strength
On loving properly
And living well.
I hope they find me destitute
All my wealth given
All my kindness shared,
That all I leave behind are ashes.
That nothing was saved for a rainy day
But that I gave it all,
Everyday –
And that in the end there's nothing left.

Girls Like Me
Hustling in silence
But making it happen.
No drama, no crazy,
Just stone cold rationality.
Appeal wrapped in reliability,
Vulnerability decorated with confidence.
Not seeking attention,
Just seeking to shatter expectations.
Hard to find, hard to impress,
Impossible to replace –
But the poets stay fairly silent
When it comes to girls like me.

Close Your Eyes
Eyes that once twinkled
With mischief –
Eyes that were warm
With love.
Eyes that have grown weary
Of life's frailties –
Eyes that I will miss dearly.
So, my dear, close your eyes,
And the next time they open
You'll see paradise.

Everything and Nothing
I want to do everything,
See the beautiful, secret places,
Explore the world,
Love and make love
Across the globe.
I want to do nothing,
Just enjoy the sunset
From my porch,
Quiet in the sense
Of loving everything I have.
I want to do everything and nothing,
With someone who's excited
To do everything and nothing with me.

Walk

If you're all in
I'll walk the burning deserts;
If you're sure of me
I'll walk continents for you –
If you're bringing it all
I'll walk through the fires of hell,
I'll walk ten thousand miles
Just to make you smile –
But if you're not sure
Then I'll just walk away.

Someday Looking Back
I hope I've loved
The way I wanted,
As much as I can;
I hope I've laughed
So hard it hurts,
More than I have cried.
I hope I've done things
Bravely, fearlessly, unselfishly,
That even one person says
They are better off because of me;
I hope that I've had passion,
Given heart changing pleasure,
And that I have no regrets
Someday looking back.

Irresistible

I don't want enough,
I don't want to be
Merely satisfied,
I don't want something that
I am simply choosing –
I want something that
Disrupts my subconscious with yearning,
Something that draws me in
Despite my defiance,
I want something
That I cannot resist.

Resistance

The tenacity needed
To resist the pressures,
To turn away from distractions
That could lure me off track.
The times that I defied the odds,
Conquering demons,
Seeing others find ways to cope,
But I didn't cope, I battled,
Building resistance,
Until I was stronger
Than the shit that tried
To get the best of me.

Woman Enough

I can dominate a room
Overpower those who doubt me,
Move mountains that stand before me –
Loudmouthed like a sailor.
I lack domestic niceties,
Not especially refined,
And some will say I'm not feminine.
But I walk with confidence,
Laugh with sincerity,
Have a heart purified by fire,
I make my own money,
And I make my own rules,
Take away everything I have
And I still have enough,
You can strip me bare
And find me shameless –
And I'm woman enough for you.

Indifference

Passion burns away,
Turns into complacency –
Urgency fades,
Replaced with neglect.
Waking up with ardor and impatience,
But becomes second thought, apathy.
When vehement desire burns out
And languishes into passivity.
The heart no longer racing,
The skin no longer tingling,
The craving no longer in the bones –
When the effort ceases
And becomes lazy
And the love becomes indifference.

Greatest Fear
My greatest fear
That I'll finally be loved
The way I've always wanted
But that I'll be too scared
To believe I'm loved that way
And won't give in to it.

Flowers

I should send myself
Some flowers,
With a note
To remind myself
Of who I am.
Celebrate my strength,
Comfort my own hurts,
Remind myself that I'm the daughter
Of the strong woman who raised me.
Flowers to cheer me
With the colorful fragrance
Of life and happiness
That is still inside of me –
I'm not waiting for
Someone else to show me,
I should send myself some flowers.

Love Story
The moments of triumph,
The beautiful things to be seen,
The challenges that are rewarded,
The milestones we achieve,
The things that give life meaning –
Tied together with the ribbons
Of a love story,
Of a cheerleader, a confidante,
A lover and a best friend,
To multiply the joys.
Without it, life could be full,
But love makes it meaningful –
It does not dimmish the individual
But amplifies and shines a light,
Becomes a fuel, a reflection,
A daily refreshment –
Why every heart is craving
A love story.

Retreat

I can lay it all
On the line for you;
Offer you everything
That there is of me;
But if you will not
Meet me there
In the chaos and
In the wild madness,
In the passionate fall,
Then I will take my heart
And retreat.

Difference

You can love
But not make a commitment.
You can love
But have no intentions.
You can love
Without making promises.
You can love
Without giving yourself –
But doing all those things
Is what makes the difference.

Both

I can go to battle,
And I can get on my knees;
I can carry the weight of the world,
And I can let it all go;
I can be as strong as iron,
And as delicate as a flower;
I can chill you with my rationality,
And amaze you with my generosity;
I can repel you with my edges,
And seduce you with my curves.
I can be a warrior or a goddess,
I can be a recluse or a hero –
I am always a woman who can be both.

Neglected
I learned to bloom
Under the shadow
Of neglect –
An unwatered flower
Growing in the shade,
Against the odds.
How I might thrive,
If I'm cherished,
If the warmth of love
Shines down on me.

Personas
The images we craft
To intrigue bystanders,
To impress onlookers
Who don't even know us.
The facades we construct,
The effigies we create
To collect worthless accolades,
When they pale compared
To who we really are.

Stupid Enough

To think that I
Can change the world,
That I can be the difference,
That no dream is ever too big,
That nothing is impossible.
To think that I
Can get the best for myself
That I can give the best of me
Without fear to someone worthy.
I'm still stupid enough
To believe I can inspire hope,
Make an impact,
To think I can disrupt the status quo.

COVID-19

They can lock us up
But they can't protect us –
Life still goes on
In quarantine –
People falling in and out of love,
Having babies, dying of other things.
People are still getting addicted,
People are still chasing their dreams,
Some people are falling into madness,
And others are perpetrating schemes.
Loneliness makes some people desperate,
And it drives others to build an empire –
For some, the lock down drives their ambition,
For others, it has extinguished their fire.
I took the challenge and said "bring it on,"
Because I can't be convinced to live in fear,
And I built some great things I am proud of –
They can lock me up but they can't ruin my year.

Consistency

I do what I say I'll do,
And I'm what I say I am –
Unvarying, unwavering,
Boring and stable.
I'm no erratic thrill,
No capricious game –
I move forward
In rationality.
I lack the passionate excitement
Of unpredictability.
I'm dependable,
There's not much mystery –
But you can believe in me,
And my relentless consistency.

Straight Talk
Girls that want praise,
To be told that they
Are stronger and more beautiful
Than they really are –
I want to be respected,
Admired honestly,
Pushed to become better,
And told directly
When I'm not being as good
As I should be –
And that's one way I'll know
It's real love.

Harmony
I've made an art
Of consistency –
I've blended rationality
With the sensuous –
I've masterfully fused
Stoicism and vulnerability –
I've honed the ability
To be both dependable and adventurous.
Passion and practicality
Have joined in perfect harmony
Inside of me.

Lonely

I have never felt
More alone
Than the moments here
Where I wasn't alone
But so lonely.
And now I'll be alone,
And I'm nervous
And a little scared
And if I wake up at 3am
I'll be by myself,
But I don't think I'll be lonely.

Ready

For the rewards I've earned
And for the fresh dreams to grow,
For new adventures
And for adversity –
For the opportunity to serve,
For the purpose within me,
For the love of a lifetime.
To wake up each day
Ready for extraordinary,
Ready to reject average,
Ready to build a life, a legacy,
A love that shakes and rebuilds me –
I'm ready.

Hurt Feelings
It stings, just a little
And it's hard to admit,
But I cannot deny
And I can close my eyes
But it doesn't change
That my feelings are hurt.

Consolation Prize

I can beat the odds
And beat the competition
With my hands tied –
I can out-do,
I can out perform,
And I can do it
With a smile –
I can shine like a raging fire
When everyone else is ashes,
But all I get is the consolation prize.

Right Now

If you're going to build with me
Let's take our time,
If you're going to dream with me
Let's grow them day by day,
If you're going to create a life with me
Let's take it slow and do it right,
But if you're going to break me
Just do it right now.

Waiting

They will show up,
With pretty words
To try to turn my head –
They'll try to capture
My heart and my freedom,
Take advantage of my weaknesses,
Prey on my capabilities –
But I am waiting,
Committed and determined,
For the love that's meant for me.

Bullied

The peer pressure
I never caved into
Made them want to punish me –
There were bruises on the outside
And scars inside they couldn't see –
The mockery, the jeering,
The public pain and ridicule,
I was a loser and an outcast,
And I refused to be like them.
Keeping my head high,
They never saw my tears.
But those trials that I faced,
Made me who I am today –
I've proven to myself
And anyone who saw me then
That I will not exchange my worth
For public acceptance.

ANNA FARLEY

Average

Common days,
Ordinary lifestyle,
Mediocre progress,
Average love –
I've come too far
And sacrificed too much
To settle for anything
That could be called average.

Brave

I was scared
But did it anyway;
Stepped outside of myself
And embraced a courage
That I didn't think I had –
I stripped myself bare
Of ancient expectations
And reached for freedom,
And all of the fear
That comes with freedom –
And I learned that I'm bravest
When my hands are shaking –
That my courage comes
Sometimes in shallow breaths –
That who I am, and my dreams,
That the life I want to live
Have made me brave enough.

Endure

No pain is too great
If I can see my purpose –
No torment too much
When my vision is clear –
If I can see
Past the tribulation
My will remains strong,
And my eyes fixed on my goal.
If I can see past the torture
To what I am striving to reach,
My affliction becomes strategic,
And I can endure anything.

What Makes Me Strong
Because I am joyful
Even in sadness.
Because I am generous
Even in need.
Because I am kind
Even when provoked.
Because I am rational
Even when I am hurt.
Because I am brave
Even when I am scared.
Because I am committed
Even when I'm unsure.
Because I am patient
Even when I am desperate.

ANNA FARLEY

Never Crazy
They say they want
Crazy in love,
But I don't want crazy
Or to ever be crazy –
I want peace in love,
Adventure and excitement,
Freedom and fidelity,
Consistency and rationality –
I want to be joyful in love,
And maybe even wild,
But never crazy.

Never Enough

I ache with a smile,
Confident only when I'm alone,
Paranoid always that
For someone else, I'm not enough.
That for someone else
I could never satisfy –
That with someone
I cannot fill their need.
That whatever I am
And everything I've become
Could never be enough –
That I'll be betrayed, forgotten
Or abandoned because
Even at my best
What if I am not enough.

My Fire

I am searing with desire,
Ablaze with passion,
Lighting up the night
And even the day –
Flickering with promise
And as certain as the sun.
A torrid, white hot flame
Of love and pleasure,
So, come dance in my flames,
But don't play with my fire.

Afterthought
The way I feel
When I know
I'm not a priority
But that I'm just
An afterthought to you.

Gone

Took it for granted,
Didn't think we could lose it,
Didn't protect it
With everything we had.
Let it get taken
In exchange for something
That turned out to be hollow.
And once gone,
We might have to die
To ever get it back.

What I Thought
I will give you everything
Anything you could ask –
The freedom,
The patience,
The unconditional love –
And if in the end, I'm not the one
Then maybe this was never
What I thought it was.

Flashlight
I was everything
But it wasn't what you wanted;
It was like you'd been
Handed the moon,
But all you really wanted
Was a flashlight.

Even Though

I wouldn't be me
If you hadn't seen something –
I wouldn't be standing on this soil
If it wasn't for you –
So even though we are parting,
Remember that so much of
Everything I am
Is partly because of you.

Shining Hard

You might find me
Alone and badly beaten,
Ravaged by challenge,
Tormented by uncertainty –
Shaken and shivering,
Maybe tears in my eyes,
But you'll find me, steadfast,
Shining hard from the inside.

Decisive

I've arrived
At the culmination
Of my courage,
My clarity,
My capability –
I've discovered,
In this season of maturity,
My vision, my worthiness –
I'm decisive, determined
And I'm daring
To build the future
I've been dreaming of.

Loosely

Speaking meaningful words
With emptiness behind them,
To persuade,
To dominate,
To regain control –
But I'm done
And will not use words
Loosely anymore.

Best of Me

The past has taken
My innocence,
It has taken away
The youthful colors
Of my hair,
It has taken my patience
And tested it and tried it
And given it back to me
A little worse for wear,
The past has taken
My foolish mistakes,
And more than a little
Of my stubborn pride,
But it's the future
That will get the best of me.

Cry Alone

The days are rarely
Tougher than me,
And nights alone
Don't often make me sad –
I'm brave enough
To see this through
And I'm strong enough
To sometimes cry alone.

More Than This
Working in monotony
Just to pay the bills,
To pass my leisure hours
Watching make believe,
Resting in stress
And waking in exhaustion,
In an endless cycle
Of just passing another day –
We were made for more than this,
And this will never be enough for me.

Choosing

I gave my younger self
Over to the expectations,
I used the playbook
And played it well –
But somewhere I found
In the moment between life and death
A desire for something different,
For dreams that cannot be
Checked off a list,
But must be felt in the heart –
Maybe I won't live my life
The way others choose,
But I'm choosing a life
That in death I'll never regret.

The Man She Needs

Men who want the dream girl,
A goddess, a woman who can do battle,
A rock, a soft place,
A refuge and a fortress,
A woman who can inspire
Both arousal and security;
The men who want a woman
Who can do it all –
Only to find her
And then he can't
Be the man that she needs.

The Storm

Maybe we give the storm
More credit than it's due,
By fearing it before it comes –
Because so often we stand
Taking the beating of its fury
With more fortitude than we ever
Knew we had –
And we come out the other side,
Maybe damaged, but refreshed,
Purified by the lashing,
And realizing that indecision
Is what actually makes us afraid,
Not the storm.

Walls
You came in and with
Relentless patience,
You tore down all my walls –
And now I must rebuild,
Higher and stronger,
So no one ever sees behind them
Ever again.

Losses

It isn't the money
Or the bands of gold
That I count as losses
As I move on from this –
It's the years of my youth
That I can't ever get back –
It's the peace of mind I had
When I believed I was enough,
Will I ever have that again?
It's the confidence I once had
As I collect the scraps of my pride
And wonder how my life got to this –
I don't count as a loss
Anything that can be reclaimed,
But those things I've lost forever,
The losses I'm counting today.

What Some People Call Love
Control, obsession,
Desperation and jealousy –
Hot headed passion
And romantic bribery –
It is bewildering
What some people call love
These days.

Confuse

Let us not mistake
Someone else's fear of change
As love –
Let us not confuse
Their unwillingness to do better
As commitment.

Goals

To live with such passion,
Such intent,
To blaze a trail so bright,
That in the end even death
Fails to snuff out the fire,
A legacy that makes the devil tremble,
And a flame that
Continues to burn bright,
Long after the bones are dust.

Fresh

It's more than just new sheets
And new pictures on the wall,
The ways that things feel fresh –
It's having learned
From my mistakes,
Knowing I won't make them again.
It's forgiving myself for failing,
And for dreams I gave up on,
Committing to a new life.
It's knowing that I know better
And will do better –
Everyday from now on.

Up From Here
I suffered, I cried,
I laid awake in bed at night –
I feared myself,
And feared the world,
And my vision had been blurred –
I paid the price,
I paid my dues,
I have earned what is now clear,
I made a choice, I had to choose,
And now it's only up from here.

More, A King

Girls looking for "prince charming"
To sweep them off their feet,
Charm and romance
To fill every moment -
I want a partner,
Love, and more than love,
I need more than a prince,
I had to find a king.

Watch Me

They think I won't,
That I'll conform,
That I'm not brave enough
To stand all alone.
They think that I'll do
Whatever everyone does,
They don't believe
That I'll go my own way.
They have their opinions,
But I'll shatter their illusions,
When they watch me.

ANNA FARLEY

Civil Disobedience

There is beauty
In the disobedience –
The courage to be
Willing to stand alone;
The resolve to accept
The consequences,
However dire,
Knowing that liberty and life
Will acknowledge you as a hero.

Praise

There are no stories,
No songs written,
About the ones who gave up,
Who backed down,
Who surrendered when
All that was good was on the line –
There are no heroic statues
To moments when safety
Triumphed over bravery,
Over protecting liberty –
There are no legends written
About self-righteous pawns
Who gave up everything
To save only their comfort –
The weak will have their day,
But the brave will make history,
Be legendary, leave a legacy
That generations will praise.

Good and Evil

It is not a virus or vaccine
That we are at war with –
Nor should it be each other,
To hate our own brother
For choosing a different path –
It is a war over freedom and oppression,
Of servitude to the state
Or terrifying freedom –
A war over darkness and light,
Over truth and humanity,
Over a future worth living for –
It is a war of good and evil,
And there is no way in hell
That evil will ever win.

Deserted

If I am going to be deserted
By friends who once loved me
Because some bought and paid for
Celebrity told them I am to blame,
Then I'll take it on the chin,
And I'll hold my head high,
Because my convictions can't be bought
Even to spare a broken heart –
I can be abandoned or forsaken
But I will not be ashamed
To stand alone for liberty.

Papers

They want to see my papers,
Papers to authorize my actions,
That designate me as compliant,
Safe and submissive –
But I'm afraid that I don't have them
Because I won't bend my knee
To the irrational and power hungry
Rulers in authority.
To be fair, and I will say it,
They can all go fuck themselves,
Because the freedom that I exercise
Is rooted in my humanity.

Crazy

They would call me crazy
If I turned to unproven,
Untested, uninformed,
Misunderstood,
Mistaken,
Experimental,
Extreme,
Uncertain, unknowable,
Unapproved treatments
To cure anything wrong with me –
But now they call me crazy,
Because I won't.

Warrior

They liked me better
When they admired me
For all the cheerfulness,
For the simplicity,
For the fun –
They do not like
My fire,
My steadfast refusal,
My uncompromising resolve,
They don't like the warrior in me.

When

When has force
Been celebrated by posterity?
When have those who silence others
Been viewed later as heroes?
When has history been celebrated
For oppression of liberty?
When has persuasion through fear
Been regarded as a virtue?

In the Mirror
In the mirror
I no longer see
The girl I was at twenty –
This new reflection
Shows maturity,
And some nuisance grey and white –
I see reminders
Of the girlishness I once had,
But it is overwhelmed,
More and more,
By lessons I've learned –
But despite these signs
Of age and decline,
I'm so proud of what I see
In the mirror.

Golden Hair
Decades, life,
The strife and the victory,
Seconds passing slowly,
But the years racing by –
The beautiful moments
Stringing the struggles together –
Trying to break my spirit,
But I'm still who I was
All those years ago
Back when I still had
Girlish hopes and golden hair.

Monster in Me

Inside of me there is a monster
Who I've come well to know,
It torments me in my darkness
But I've tamed it well –
I let it torture only me,
I don't let it see the light,
And I wrestle with this demon,
One on one from time to time –
It has it's fated pattern
Written in the stars
That I'll spend my mortal life
Subduing the monster in me.

New Dreams
Played out,
There's nothing left here
Of the dream it used to be.
This soil has served its purpose
But now it's time is done –
Some dreams don't come true,
But some do,
Then they grow old
And die away.
New dreams are born,
And we stay young
When we chase them
And make our lives a fertile
Place for them to grow.

The Unknown

I'd trade all my dollars
For just one dream come true,
Give up all I have known
To discover my hopes –
I have taken leaps
Into the unknown,
Seeking adventure,
Searching for passion,
Chasing the fullest life,
And believe that I'll find it.

Meant to Be

Trading these city lights
For the stars in the sky at night,
Trading the southern sun
For a white Christmas –
I'm trading this Lone Star
For a million Midwest stars
And I'm trading my girlhood dream
For what is meant to be.

Somewhere North of Here
I only want adventure,
I only want anticipation,
A future that is bright –
Scared isn't even the word,
Terrified –
But hope is stronger,
Love is braver,
Excitement is more persuasive –
I only want it all in life
And I'll find it somewhere north of here.

Purged
The parts of me
That used to self-destruct,
The parts that
Thrived in the dark side of me,
They are gone –
The light has taken over,
And it has purged the darkness.

Clean Slate
Little things
Pile up
Create guilt,
Fuel shame –
Undealt, unforgiven,
Self-loathing,
Circular life –
Breaking free,
Fresh start,
No guilt,
Only light,
Takes work,
So worthwhile,
Pure freedom,
Clean slate.

New Book

It isn't a new chapter,
It's a whole new story,
A new beginning,
The start of a new life –
It's a new place,
A better me,
Every new possibility
Of a better ending this time –
It's a new plot line,
Where I can be my own hero,
Because I saved myself
From who I was becoming,
And gave myself a new book
Where I can be who I'm meant to be.

ANNA FARLEY

Leaving Easy
A thousand small pleasures,
Dreams come true,
Wishes that became memories,
A place where roots had grown –
But the things unfulfilled,
The dreams still untouched,
The ideals I've been chasing
That I can finally see,
The things that take a good life
And make it breathtaking,
Those things make leaving easy.

I'd like to feature a special selection here with the permission of my mom, Rhonda Farley, of a poem that my late father, George Farley, wrote to her on the night that I was born.

Rhonda,
I couldn't sleep at all last night
I was just thinking about you,
So a poet's pen
I grasped again
And praying rhymes may well unfold,
I tried to bear my heart and soul…
To trace and rhyme, the thoughts again.
That say 'I love you'
My wife, my friend…
But the poet's words are vain and bold,
And rhymes won't measure
The place you hold
And useless words can't ever say
Of the things within,
I felt that day,
When God's gift showed her little head
And joy filled tears I later shed,
An eight-pound one-ounce bundle of joy,
It was no matter if not a boy!
So, with these roses
I now uphold
The failed attempts,
In iambic pent,
That fail the poet's goal…

84